JOSEPH the DREAMER

Publishing House
St. Louis

CONCORDIA PUBLISHING HOUSE,
3558 South Jefferson Avenue,
Saint Louis, Missouri 63118.

© Copyright 1983 Palm Tree Press Ltd.

ISBN 0 86208 026 6

U.S.A. Edition by
Concordia Publishing House
St. Louis, MO USA 1983.

Printed by E. T. Heron, Essex and London, England.

JOSEPH the DREAMER

Retold from Scripture
by Barbara McMeekin
and illustrated
by Arthur Baker

This is the story of Joseph,
who lived in a land called Canaan.

Would you believe
he had eleven brothers!

Ten were older than he was,
and just one was younger.

The oldest was called Reuben,
and the youngest was called Benjamin.

Their father was called Jacob.

Every day Jacob would gather
his twelve sons around him
and talk to them about God.

Everyone in this large family
   had to work very hard
   because there were so many
   mouths to feed.

The older brothers
   worked in the fields,
   looking after their father's sheep.

When Joseph was seventeen,
  he began to go along
  to the fields with his brothers.

He wanted to help too.

But his brothers
  were not too happy about that.

"Oh no!"
  they would moan to each other,
  "Do we have to take Joseph along?"

You see,
  Joseph was his father's favorite son,
  and the others were jealous.

Jacob loved Joseph so much
  that he gave him a special coat.

It was made of lots of small pieces,
  all stitched together,
  and it had beautiful long sleeves.

When the brothers
   saw this beautiful coat,
   you can imagine
   how they grumbled
   and groaned among themselves.

"Why does Dad
   make such a fuss over him?"
   asked one.

"We could all do
   with a nice new coat,"
   another said.

"It doesn't suit him anyway!"
   said a third jealously.

The brothers were all very cross!

Now one night
   Joseph had a dream.

In the morning
   he jumped out of bed
   and rushed to tell his brothers.

"Listen!" he said,
   "We were all in a field,
   tying up bundles of corn.
   Then my bundle stood in the middle
   and yours bowed down to mine!"

This made the brothers very angry.

"Does that mean you think
   you are more important than we are?"
   they shouted.

Poor Joseph!

His brothers didn't like him,
   and they didn't want
   to talk to him anymore
   — especially when he announced
   that he had had another dream.

"This time," he said,
   "the sun, moon, and eleven stars
   were bowing down to me!"

Joseph's brothers
became very fed up with him
and his dreams!

One day
Jacob said to Joseph:
"Your brothers are out
looking after the sheep.
Go and see
how they are getting on,
will you?"

It was a long, dusty walk,
but after a time
Joseph saw his brothers
in the distance.

But his brothers
had seen him first. . .

"Here comes the dreamer!"
    they said.

"He's probably only come
    to spy on us
    and tell Father what we are up to.
    Let's kill him
    and throw him into this pit.
    Then we can tell Dad
    a wild beast caught him."

And so the wicked brothers plotted!

But Reuben, the oldest brother,
    knew how much
    his father loved Joseph.

"No! Don't kill him," he said,
    "we'll just throw him into the pit."

So when Joseph arrived,
 the wicked brothers
 tore off his coat
 and threw him into the pit.

"That's getting rid of him!"
 they cried,
 and off they went
 to have their lunch.

While they were eating,
 they saw some traders
 coming towards them.

The traders' camels
 were piled high with goods
 for sale in the markets of Egypt.

"Hey!" said Judah,
   "we don't really want
   to kill Joseph, do we?
   Why don't we sell him to these men?"

"Good idea!" cried the brothers.

So. . .
   when the traders came close,
   the brothers took poor Joseph
   from the pit.

Instead of rescuing him,
   they sold him to the traders.

Twenty pieces of silver
   was the price they got!

So when Reuben
    went back to the pit,
    Joseph was nowhere to be seen.

"Oh no!" Reuben gasped,
    "What shall I do?"

He called all the brothers together,
    and they hatched a plot.

They would tell their father
    a lie. . .

And this is what they did. . .

They caught hold of a goat
   and killed it.

Then they dipped
   Joseph's lovely coat
   in the blood.

They would show their father
   the coat and say:
   "Look!
   A wild animal attacked Joseph
   and killed him!"

And, of course,
   when Jacob heard the brothers' story
   he just sat down on his bed
   and cried,
   and cried,
   and cried.

In the meantime
the traders had taken Joseph to Egypt
and sold him as a slave.

The man who bought him
was called Potiphar,
and he was a captain
in the king's army.

"That lad looks good and strong,"
Potiphar thought to himself,
"I'll put him to work
in the house."

And Potiphar was quite right!
Not only was Joseph strong,
but he worked hard as well.

Potiphar was very pleased,
and put Joseph in charge
of his house
and all the servants.

Neither had God forgotten Joseph.
In His own time
God would release Joseph
from slavery
and call him to do great things.

But that is another story. . .

Note for parents:
This story may be found
in the Book of Genesis,
chapter 37.

You will enjoy the other
Palm Tree Bible Stories!

OLD TESTAMENT STORIES

NEW TESTAMENT STORIES

Watch for new titles coming!